The History of Norway

The Land of the Midnight Sun

The Geology and Geography of Norway 6

The Early Inhabitants of Norway 8

The Viking Age: Society, Culture, and Expansion 10

The Viking Age: Exploration and Colonization 12

The Viking Age: Trade and Commerce 14

The Viking Age: Religion and Mythology 16

The Christianization of Norway 18

The High Middle Ages: Consolidation and Centralization 20

The High Middle Ages: The Black Death and Its Aftermath 22

The Kalmar Union and the Union of Denmark-Norway 24

The Reformation and the Lutheran Church in Norway 26

The Age of Absolutism and the Rise of the Norwegian Identity 28

The Napoleonic Wars and the Separation from Denmark 30

The Struggle for Independence and the Union with Sweden 32

The Romantic Nationalism of the 19th Century 34

The Industrial Revolution and Urbanization 36

The Birth of Norwegian Literature and Arts 38

The Sami People and Their Struggle for Rights 40

Norway's Role in World War I 42

The Interwar Period and the Rise of Fascism 44

The German Occupation of Norway during World War II 46

The Norwegian Resistance Movement 48

The Post-War Reconstruction and Social Democracy 50

The Discovery of Oil and the Norwegian Economic Miracle 52

The Expansion of the Welfare State and Social Progressivism 54

The Norwegian Model of Democracy and Diplomacy 56

Contemporary Norway: Challenges and Prospects 58

Conclusion 60

The Geology and Geography of Norway

Norway is located on the western portion of the Scandinavian Peninsula, which extends into the North Sea and the Norwegian Sea. It is bordered to the east by Sweden and to the north by Finland and Russia. Norway has a total area of about 385,000 square kilometers, making it the 67th largest country in the world.

The geology of Norway is varied and complex. The country is situated at the edge of the Eurasian Plate and the North American Plate, which has resulted in the formation of several mountain ranges, including the Scandinavian Mountains, which run through the central part of the country. These mountains were formed as a result of tectonic activity and the collision of the two plates.

Norway has a coastline that stretches for over 25,000 kilometers, including numerous fjords and islands. The country's longest fjord, Sognefjord, is located on the western coast and is over 200 kilometers long. Other notable fjords include Hardangerfjord, Geirangerfjord, and Nærøyfjord.

Norway also has several large lakes, including Mjøsa, which is the largest lake in Norway and the fourth-largest lake in Europe. The country is also home to several rivers, including the Glomma, which is the longest river in Norway, stretching over 600 kilometers.

Norway's terrain is rugged and mountainous, with over 50% of the country covered by mountains and high plateaus. The highest peak in Norway is Galdhøpiggen, which stands at 2,469 meters above sea level. Other notable peaks include Glittertind, Store Skagastølstind, and Jotunheimen.

Norway is known for its rich natural resources, including oil, natural gas, minerals, and forests. The country is the world's fifth-largest exporter of oil and gas and has extensive reserves in the North Sea. Norway also has significant reserves of iron ore, copper, zinc, and other minerals.

The climate in Norway varies greatly depending on the location. The coastal areas have a mild and humid climate, while the interior and northern parts of the country have a colder, subarctic climate. The warmest temperatures are typically found in the south and southeast, while the coldest temperatures are found in the high plateaus and mountains in the interior.

Overall, Norway's geography and geology have played a significant role in shaping the country's history and culture. The rugged terrain and vast natural resources have allowed Norway to become a major player in industries such as oil and gas, mining, and forestry, while the unique fjords and mountains have made the country a popular destination for tourism and outdoor recreation.

The Early Inhabitants of Norway

The earliest inhabitants of Norway were hunter-gatherers who arrived in the region during the last ice age, around 10,000 BCE. These early people lived along the coastline and relied on fishing, hunting, and gathering for their survival. They left behind little evidence of their existence, but archaeologists have found stone tools, animal bones, and other artifacts that suggest their way of life.

Around 4,000 BCE, the climate began to warm, and the glaciers began to recede, allowing for a more diverse range of plant and animal life to flourish. This led to the development of agriculture, and by 2,000 BCE, the first farmers had settled in Norway. These early farmers cultivated crops such as wheat, barley, and rye, and raised livestock such as cattle, sheep, and goats. They also began to build permanent settlements, which were typically located near the coast or along major rivers.

Around 500 BCE, the Nordic Bronze Age began, and with it came a new wave of cultural and technological developments. During this time, bronze weapons and tools became more common, and long-distance trade networks began to emerge. People in Norway began to specialize in certain crafts, such as metalworking, pottery, and textiles.

The Iron Age began in Norway around 500 CE, and with it came significant social and political changes. The early Iron Age was marked by the emergence of chiefdoms, which were organized around powerful leaders who controlled land, resources, and labor. These leaders were often buried in elaborate tombs, which served as symbols of their power and status.

The Viking Age began in Norway around 800 CE and lasted until the 11th century. During this time, Norway became a major player in European politics and culture. The Vikings were skilled sailors and traders who traveled throughout Europe and beyond, establishing trade networks, raiding other settlements, and settling in new areas. The Vikings also developed a rich culture, which included religion, art, and literature.

By the end of the Viking Age, Norway had become a highly stratified society, with a small ruling elite controlling most of the country's resources. The majority of the population was made up of farmers and laborers who worked the land for their overlords.

Overall, the early inhabitants of Norway were a diverse group of people who adapted to the changing environment and developed new technologies and social structures over time. Their legacy can still be seen today in the country's rich cultural traditions and unique way of life.

The Viking Age: Society, Culture, and Expansion

The Viking Age in Norway lasted from approximately the 8th to the 11th centuries. During this time, Norway was a highly stratified society, with a ruling elite at the top, and farmers and laborers making up the majority of the population. The Vikings were skilled sailors, traders, and warriors who established trade networks, raided other settlements, and settled in new areas.

Society during the Viking Age was organized around powerful chieftains and rulers who controlled land, resources, and labor. The elite lived in large halls, which served as centers of power and prestige. These halls were often decorated with elaborate carvings, tapestries, and other works of art.

The Viking Age was also marked by significant technological advancements. The Vikings were skilled shipbuilders and sailors, and they developed highly efficient longships that allowed them to travel great distances and carry out raids and conquests. They also developed advanced ironworking techniques, which allowed them to create stronger weapons and tools.

Religion played an important role in Viking society, and the Vikings worshipped a pantheon of gods and goddesses, including Odin, Thor, and Freyja. They believed in an afterlife, and often buried their dead with valuable possessions and weapons.

The Vikings also had a rich literary and artistic culture. They created epic poems and stories, such as the Saga of the Volsungs and Beowulf, which told tales of heroic warriors and powerful gods. They also created intricate metalwork, jewelry, and textiles, which were highly prized for their beauty and craftsmanship.

During the Viking Age, Norway expanded its influence and territory through trade and conquest. The Vikings established trade networks throughout Europe and beyond, and established settlements in areas such as Iceland, Greenland, and Vinland (present-day Newfoundland). They also carried out raids on other settlements, and conquered and settled in areas such as England, Scotland, and Ireland.

Despite their reputation as raiders and warriors, the Vikings also engaged in peaceful trade and diplomacy. They established diplomatic relationships with other kingdoms and often intermarried with local rulers.

Overall, the Viking Age was a time of significant cultural, technological, and political development in Norway. The Vikings' legacy can still be seen today in the country's rich cultural traditions and unique way of life.

The Viking Age: Exploration and Colonization

During the Viking Age, Norway experienced a significant period of exploration and colonization. The Vikings were skilled sailors and navigators, and they established trade networks, raided other settlements, and settled in new areas.

One of the most notable achievements of the Vikings was their exploration of the North Atlantic Ocean. The Vikings were the first Europeans to reach North America, nearly 500 years before Christopher Columbus. Around the year 1000 CE, Leif Erikson led an expedition to what is now Newfoundland, Canada, and established a settlement known as Vinland.

In addition to Vinland, the Vikings also established settlements in Iceland and Greenland. These settlements were established primarily for farming, and the Vikings brought with them livestock and crops such as barley and rye. The Vikings also established trade networks with other settlements in the North Atlantic, including those in modern-day Ireland and Scotland.

The Vikings were also successful colonizers in other parts of Europe. They established settlements in England, Scotland, and Ireland, and controlled large parts of what is now modern-day France. The Vikings also established a settlement in what is now Russia, known as the Kievan Rus.

The Viking approach to colonization was unique in that they did not simply conquer and assimilate other cultures. Instead, they often established diplomatic relationships and intermarried with local rulers. This approach allowed for a blending of cultures and facilitated peaceful trade and commerce.

One of the most significant impacts of Viking colonization was the spread of the Old Norse language. The Vikings spoke a language known as Old Norse, which was the ancestor of modern-day Scandinavian languages. The Vikings' colonization of other areas led to the spread of Old Norse, which had a lasting impact on the languages and cultures of Europe.

Overall, the Viking Age was a period of significant exploration and colonization for Norway. The Vikings' skills as sailors, navigators, and traders allowed them to establish settlements and trade networks throughout Europe and the North Atlantic. The Vikings' approach to colonization was unique and facilitated peaceful trade and cultural exchange. The Vikings' legacy can still be seen today in the languages, cultures, and traditions of the areas they settled.

The Viking Age: Trade and Commerce

The Viking Age was marked by significant trade and commerce, as the Vikings established trade networks throughout Europe and beyond. The Vikings were skilled sailors, navigators, and traders, and they transported goods such as furs, timber, metals, and slaves.

One of the most important trade routes during the Viking Age was the "Volga Trade Route," which connected the Vikings with the Islamic world. The Vikings traveled from Scandinavia down the Volga River to trade with the Khazars, who controlled much of the trade between Europe and Asia. The Vikings exchanged furs, slaves, and amber for silver, silks, and spices.

The Vikings also established trade networks throughout the North Atlantic, including in Iceland, Greenland, and Vinland (present-day Newfoundland). They traded goods such as walrus ivory, sealskins, and fish with other settlements in the region. The Vikings also established trade networks with other European kingdoms, including those in England, Scotland, and Ireland.

The Vikings were also skilled craftsmen, and they produced high-quality goods such as metalwork, jewelry, and textiles. These goods were highly prized for their beauty and craftsmanship and were often traded for other goods or used as gifts for diplomatic purposes.

One of the most significant impacts of Viking trade was the spread of Christianity. The Vikings traded with Christian kingdoms such as England and France, and through these trade networks, they were exposed to Christian ideas and beliefs. This exposure led to the eventual conversion of many Vikings to Christianity.

The Vikings also played an important role in the development of medieval towns and cities. They established trading posts and settlements in areas such as York, Dublin, and Novgorod, which eventually grew into major commercial centers. The Vikings brought with them new ideas and technologies, such as coinage and weights and measures, which facilitated the growth of commerce and trade.

Overall, the Viking Age was a period of significant trade and commerce for Norway. The Vikings' skills as sailors, navigators, and traders allowed them to establish trade networks throughout Europe and beyond. The Vikings' legacy can still be seen today in the development of medieval towns and cities and in the cultural and economic exchanges that occurred during this time.

The Viking Age: Religion and Mythology

Religion and mythology played an important role in Viking society during the Viking Age. The Vikings worshipped a pantheon of gods and goddesses, and their beliefs and rituals were closely tied to their daily lives.

The Vikings believed in a variety of gods and goddesses, including Odin, Thor, and Freyja. These gods were associated with different aspects of nature and life, and each had their own distinct personality and characteristics.

Odin was the chief god in the Viking pantheon, and he was associated with wisdom, knowledge, and war. He was often depicted as a one-eyed man, and he carried a spear and a pair of ravens, which he used to gather information.

Thor was the god of thunder and lightning, and he was associated with strength and protection. He was often depicted carrying a hammer, which he used to control the weather and protect his followers.

Freyja was the goddess of love, fertility, and war. She was often depicted as a beautiful woman, and she wore a cloak of falcon feathers, which allowed her to transform into a bird.

The Vikings believed in an afterlife, and they buried their dead with valuable possessions and weapons, which they believed would be useful in the afterlife. They also believed in the existence of different realms, including Asgard (the home of the gods) and Helheim (the realm of the dead).

The Vikings also had a rich literary and artistic culture, which was closely tied to their religion and mythology. They created epic poems and stories, such as the Saga of the Volsungs and Beowulf, which told tales of heroic warriors and powerful gods. They also created intricate metalwork, jewelry, and textiles, which often featured depictions of gods and goddesses.

Despite their beliefs in a pantheon of gods and goddesses, the Vikings were also open to the influence of other religions. As they expanded their trade networks and settled in new areas, they were exposed to new ideas and beliefs, including Christianity. Many Vikings eventually converted to Christianity, and the influence of Christian ideas can be seen in Viking art and literature from the later Viking Age.

Overall, religion and mythology played a significant role in Viking society during the Viking Age. The Vikings' beliefs in a pantheon of gods and goddesses, as well as their rich literary and artistic culture, had a lasting impact on the history and culture of Norway and beyond.

The Christianization of Norway

The Christianization of Norway was a gradual process that occurred over several centuries. The Vikings had been exposed to Christianity through their trade networks and interactions with Christian kingdoms, but it wasn't until the 11th century that Christianity began to gain a foothold in Norway.

One of the earliest Christian influences in Norway was the Irish monk St. Brendan, who is said to have visited Norway in the 6th century. He may have brought with him Christian ideas and teachings, but there is little concrete evidence of his influence.

The first significant attempt to Christianize Norway came in the late 10th century when the Norwegian king Olaf Tryggvason returned from exile in England and began to promote Christianity. Olaf was a Christian himself and believed that the conversion of Norway to Christianity would help unify the country and bring it closer to other Christian kingdoms in Europe.

Olaf used a combination of persuasion and force to promote Christianity in Norway. He built churches and promoted Christian clergy, and he also destroyed pagan temples and idols. His efforts met with mixed success, and he was eventually killed in battle in 1000 CE.

After Olaf's death, his successors continued to promote Christianity, but progress was slow. It wasn't until the reign of King Olaf II, also known as St. Olaf, that Christianity gained a stronger foothold in Norway. St. Olaf was a devout Christian who promoted the building of churches and the establishment of Christian clergy. He also led a campaign against pagan practices, which helped to further promote the spread of Christianity.

Despite St. Olaf's efforts, the Christianization of Norway was not complete until the 12th century. The Norwegian church was established as an independent entity from the church in Rome in the mid-11th century, and a number of Norwegian bishops were appointed. The country was still largely rural, and the process of converting the entire population to Christianity was slow and gradual.

The Christianization of Norway had a profound impact on the country's culture and society. It brought Norway closer to other Christian kingdoms in Europe, and it helped to unify the country under a common religion. It also led to the development of a distinct Norwegian church and religious culture, which has had a lasting impact on the country's history and identity.

Overall, the Christianization of Norway was a gradual process that took several centuries to complete. It was driven by a combination of political and religious factors, and it had a profound impact on the country's culture and society.

The High Middle Ages: Consolidation and Centralization

The High Middle Ages in Norway saw a period of consolidation and centralization as the country's power became increasingly centralized under the control of the monarchy. This period was marked by the growth of towns and cities, the expansion of trade and commerce, and the strengthening of the Norwegian church.

One of the most significant events of the High Middle Ages in Norway was the reign of King Harald Hardrada. Harald was a skilled warrior and military commander who led Norway through a period of expansion and consolidation. He conquered parts of Denmark and Sweden and established a strong central government in Norway. He also promoted Christianity and built churches throughout the country.

The High Middle Ages saw the growth of towns and cities in Norway, which became important centers of trade and commerce. Bergen, which had been founded as a trading post in the early Middle Ages, grew into a major commercial center during this period. The city became a hub for the trade of fish, furs, and timber, and it was a gateway for trade with other European kingdoms.

The growth of towns and cities in Norway also led to the emergence of a new merchant class. These merchants became wealthy through trade and commerce, and they played an important role in the country's economy and politics.

The Norwegian church also became increasingly powerful during the High Middle Ages. The establishment of the Norwegian church as an independent entity from the church in Rome in the 11th century helped to strengthen its authority and influence. The church became a major landowner and played an important role in the country's politics and culture.

The High Middle Ages also saw significant developments in Norwegian art and architecture. The Stave churches, which are unique wooden churches found throughout Norway, were built during this period. These churches were highly ornate and decorated with intricate carvings and designs.

Overall, the High Middle Ages in Norway were marked by consolidation and centralization as the country's power became increasingly centralized under the control of the monarchy. The growth of towns and cities, the expansion of trade and commerce, and the strengthening of the Norwegian church all contributed to the development of a distinct Norwegian identity and culture.

The High Middle Ages: The Black Death and Its Aftermath

The High Middle Ages in Norway were marked by a period of growth and development, but this period was abruptly interrupted by the arrival of the Black Death. The Black Death, which arrived in Norway in the mid-14th century, had a profound impact on the country's population, economy, and culture.

The Black Death was a highly contagious disease caused by the bacterium Yersinia pestis. It was spread through fleas that lived on rats, and it was transmitted to humans through bites from infected fleas. The Black Death was highly lethal, and it is estimated that it killed between 30-60% of Norway's population.

The Black Death had a significant impact on Norway's economy. The country's agriculture and trade were severely disrupted, and the shortage of labor caused by the high mortality rate led to significant inflation. The price of goods skyrocketed, and many farmers were forced to abandon their land as they could not afford to pay the high taxes.

The Black Death also had a profound impact on Norwegian society and culture. The mass deaths caused by the disease led to a sense of despair and hopelessness, and many turned to religious faith for comfort. The impact of the Black Death is reflected in the country's literature and art, which often depict scenes of death and despair.

Despite the devastation caused by the Black Death, the period following the outbreak saw significant changes in Norway's social and economic structure. The shortage of labor caused by the high mortality rate led to increased wages for workers and greater opportunities for social mobility. This led to the emergence of a new middle class, which played an important role in the country's economy and politics.

The Black Death also had a significant impact on the Norwegian church. The high mortality rate among clergy led to a shortage of priests, and this led to the development of new religious orders and the promotion of lay piety. The impact of the Black Death can still be seen today in the country's religious culture, which places a strong emphasis on individual piety and devotion.

Overall, the Black Death had a profound impact on Norway's population, economy, and culture. The high mortality rate caused by the disease led to significant changes in the country's social and economic structure, and its impact can still be seen in the country's literature, art, and religious culture.

The Kalmar Union and the Union of Denmark-Norway

The Kalmar Union, also known as the Union of Kalmar, was a political union between Denmark, Norway, and Sweden that was established in 1397. The union was created as a way to counter the growing power of the Hanseatic League, a powerful trading alliance that controlled much of the Baltic Sea trade.

Under the terms of the Kalmar Union, Denmark, Norway, and Sweden remained independent kingdoms, but they were united under a single monarch. The union was led by a monarch who was elected by a council composed of representatives from each of the member kingdoms. The monarch was responsible for overseeing the administration of the union and for representing it in foreign affairs.

The Kalmar Union was not without its problems, and there were frequent disputes between the member kingdoms. Norway, in particular, was often at a disadvantage within the union, as it was the smallest and least powerful of the three kingdoms. Despite these difficulties, the Kalmar Union lasted for more than a century, and it played an important role in the history of Scandinavia.

In 1523, Sweden broke away from the Kalmar Union and became an independent kingdom. Denmark and Norway remained united under a single monarch, but their relationship was often strained. In 1536, the Danish king Christian III implemented a series of reforms that effectively annexed Norway into the Danish kingdom.

Norway became a province of Denmark and was no longer an independent kingdom.

The union of Denmark and Norway lasted until 1814, when Norway was ceded to Sweden following the Napoleonic Wars. During this period, Denmark and Norway were ruled by a single monarch, but the two countries had separate legal systems and administrative structures.

The union of Denmark-Norway had a significant impact on Norwegian history and culture. The period saw the growth of a distinct Norwegian national identity, as the country struggled to assert its independence within the union. The union also had a profound impact on the country's economy, as it led to the growth of trade and commerce between Denmark and Norway.

Overall, the Kalmar Union and the union of Denmark-Norway played important roles in the history of Scandinavia. These unions helped to shape the political, economic, and cultural development of the region, and their legacy can still be seen today in the countries that emerged from them.

The Reformation and the Lutheran Church in Norway

The Reformation was a period of significant religious and cultural change that occurred throughout Europe in the 16th century. The movement was characterized by a rejection of many of the practices and beliefs of the Catholic Church, and it led to the establishment of new Protestant churches throughout the continent.

In Norway, the Reformation was led by the Danish king Christian III, who implemented a series of reforms that effectively abolished the Catholic Church and established the Lutheran Church as the official state religion. These reforms were implemented in 1537, and they had a significant impact on Norwegian society and culture.

The Lutheran Church quickly became the dominant religious institution in Norway, and it played an important role in shaping the country's identity and culture. The church was heavily involved in education and the dissemination of knowledge, and it played an important role in the development of the Norwegian language and literature.

The Lutheran Church in Norway was led by a bishop, who was appointed by the Danish king. The church was organized into a hierarchical structure, with bishops overseeing a network of clergy and parishioners. The church was responsible for overseeing many aspects of Norwegian society, including marriage and social welfare.

The Lutheran Church in Norway also played an important role in the country's politics. The church was closely tied to the monarchy, and it played a significant role in the development of the Norwegian state. The church was involved in the drafting of laws and the administration of justice, and it played an important role in the country's foreign affairs.

Despite its dominant role in Norwegian society, the Lutheran Church was not without its critics. There were frequent disputes between the church and the state, and there were also debates within the church itself over matters of theology and practice. These debates led to the development of different factions within the church, and they contributed to the development of a distinct Norwegian religious culture.

Overall, the Reformation and the establishment of the Lutheran Church had a profound impact on Norwegian society and culture. The church played an important role in shaping the country's identity and politics, and it remains a significant cultural institution to this day.

The Age of Absolutism and the Rise of the Norwegian Identity

The Age of Absolutism was a period of political centralization and consolidation that occurred throughout Europe in the 17th and 18th centuries. In Norway, this period was marked by the emergence of a distinct Norwegian national identity and the growth of a sense of independence from Denmark.

Under the reign of King Christian IV, who ruled Denmark and Norway from 1588 to 1648, Norway was heavily influenced by the Danish monarchy. However, the reign of Christian V, who ruled from 1670 to 1699, marked the beginning of a period of increased centralization and control from Denmark. Christian V implemented a series of reforms that strengthened the power of the monarchy and centralized control over the Norwegian government.

Despite this centralization of power, the Age of Absolutism also saw the emergence of a distinct Norwegian national identity. This identity was shaped by a growing sense of pride in Norwegian culture and history, and it was strengthened by the development of a distinct Norwegian language and literature.

The Norwegian identity was also shaped by a series of cultural movements, including the Romantic movement, which emphasized the beauty of the natural world and the importance of individual freedom and expression. This movement led to a renewed interest in Norwegian folk traditions and a celebration of Norwegian culture and history.

The Age of Absolutism also saw significant developments in the Norwegian economy. The growth of trade and commerce led to the development of a prosperous merchant class, and this class played an increasingly important role in the country's politics and society. The growth of industry and manufacturing also led to the development of new economic opportunities, particularly in the textile and timber industries.

Despite the growth of a distinct Norwegian identity and economy, Norway remained under Danish rule throughout much of the Age of Absolutism. However, the period also saw the emergence of a growing sense of Norwegian independence, which would eventually lead to the establishment of a separate Norwegian state in the 19th century.

Overall, the Age of Absolutism was a period of political centralization and consolidation, but it also saw the emergence of a distinct Norwegian national identity and the growth of a sense of independence from Denmark. These developments played an important role in shaping the country's culture, politics, and economy, and they laid the foundation for the establishment of a separate Norwegian state in the years to come.

The Napoleonic Wars and the Separation from Denmark

The Napoleonic Wars, which lasted from 1803 to 1815, had a significant impact on Norway and its relationship with Denmark. The wars were fought between France and a coalition of European powers, and they had a profound impact on the political and social structure of Europe.

Norway, which was at the time a province of Denmark, was caught up in the conflict between France and the European powers. Denmark initially remained neutral in the conflict, but in 1807, the British navy launched a surprise attack on Copenhagen and destroyed much of the Danish navy. In response to this attack, Denmark entered into an alliance with France, which placed Norway in a precarious position.

In 1814, the Napoleonic Wars came to an end with the defeat of France. As part of the peace settlement, Norway was ceded to Sweden, while Denmark retained control over its remaining territories. This separation from Denmark was a significant event in Norwegian history, and it marked the beginning of a new era of independence for the country.

The separation from Denmark was not without its challenges, however. The country was forced to negotiate a new political and economic relationship with Sweden, and there were significant differences between the two countries. Norway, for example, had a more democratic political system than Sweden, and this led to tensions between the two countries.

Despite these challenges, the separation from Denmark also brought significant benefits for Norway. The country was able to establish a separate identity and culture, and it developed a strong sense of national pride and independence. The separation also led to significant economic growth and development, as Norway was able to establish its own trade relationships and exploit its abundant natural resources.

Overall, the Napoleonic Wars and the separation from Denmark had a profound impact on Norway and its history. The wars brought significant political and social changes to Europe, and they led to the establishment of a separate Norwegian state. This separation marked the beginning of a new era in Norwegian history, and it set the stage for the country's emergence as a modern, independent nation.

The Struggle for Independence and the Union with Sweden

The separation from Denmark in 1814 marked the beginning of a new era of independence for Norway. However, this independence was short-lived, as the country was forced into a union with Sweden just a few months later.

The union with Sweden was established in 1814, after a brief period of negotiations between Norwegian and Swedish representatives. The terms of the union were established in the Treaty of Kiel, which stipulated that Norway was to be ceded to Sweden in exchange for Swedish control over several territories in northern Germany.

The union with Sweden was not without controversy, and there were significant protests and opposition to the union within Norway. Many Norwegians saw the union as a violation of their newly-won independence, and they were unhappy with the terms of the agreement. However, the union was ultimately established, and Sweden and Norway remained united for nearly a century.

The union with Sweden was marked by a number of political and social challenges. Norway, for example, had a more democratic political system than Sweden, and this led to tensions between the two countries. Norway also had a stronger sense of national identity and pride than Sweden, and this led to friction between the two nations.

Despite these challenges, the union with Sweden also brought significant benefits for Norway. The country was able to establish a stronger economy and more efficient government, and it was able to take advantage of the resources and opportunities available within the larger Swedish state.

The struggle for independence from Sweden continued throughout the 19th century, however, and there were several attempts to break away from the union. In 1905, these efforts were successful, and Norway was able to establish itself as an independent nation once again.

The struggle for independence and the union with Sweden were significant events in Norwegian history, and they helped to shape the country's identity and culture. The union with Sweden brought both benefits and challenges, and it ultimately paved the way for Norway's eventual independence in the 20th century.

The Romantic Nationalism of the 19th Century

The Romantic Nationalism of the 19th century was a cultural movement that swept across Europe, and it had a significant impact on Norway and its national identity. This movement emphasized the importance of individual freedom, national pride, and cultural expression, and it celebrated the unique history and traditions of each nation.

In Norway, the Romantic Nationalism movement was particularly strong, and it helped to shape the country's cultural and political identity. The movement was closely tied to the development of the Norwegian language and literature, and it celebrated the country's natural beauty and unique cultural traditions.

One of the most prominent figures of the Norwegian Romantic Nationalism movement was the writer Henrik Wergeland. Wergeland was a poet and playwright who celebrated Norwegian history, culture, and language in his works. He was a fierce advocate for the rights of the Norwegian people, and he helped to inspire a sense of national pride and identity among his fellow countrymen.

Another important figure in the Romantic Nationalism movement was the composer Edvard Grieg. Grieg's music was heavily influenced by Norwegian folk traditions, and it helped to create a distinct Norwegian musical identity. His music celebrated the natural beauty of Norway and the country's unique cultural heritage, and it helped to shape the way that Norwegians thought about themselves and their place in the world.

The Romantic Nationalism movement also had a significant impact on Norwegian politics. It helped to inspire a sense of national identity and pride, and it played an important role in the country's struggle for independence from Sweden. The movement was closely tied to the development of a democratic political system in Norway, and it helped to shape the country's political culture and values.

Overall, the Romantic Nationalism movement of the 19th century had a profound impact on Norway and its national identity. The movement celebrated the country's unique history, culture, and traditions, and it helped to inspire a sense of national pride and independence. The movement also played an important role in shaping Norwegian politics and culture, and it helped to lay the foundation for the country's emergence as a modern, independent nation.

The Industrial Revolution and Urbanization

The Industrial Revolution and Urbanization had a profound impact on Norway in the 19th and early 20th centuries. This period of rapid industrialization and urban growth brought significant changes to the country's economy, society, and culture.

The Industrial Revolution began in Norway in the mid-19th century, and it was marked by the development of new industries and manufacturing techniques. The country's abundant natural resources, such as timber and iron, were key factors in driving this economic growth. The growth of industry led to increased production and the creation of new jobs, and it helped to fuel economic development throughout the country.

One of the most significant effects of the Industrial Revolution in Norway was the growth of urbanization. Cities such as Oslo, Bergen, and Trondheim saw significant population growth, as people moved from rural areas to the cities in search of work and better living conditions. This urbanization had a profound impact on Norwegian society and culture, as it led to the development of new forms of social organization and cultural expression.

The growth of industry and urbanization also had a significant impact on the environment. The rapid expansion of industry and urban areas led to pollution and the degradation of natural habitats, and this had significant negative effects on the health and well-being of both people and wildlife.

Despite these challenges, the Industrial Revolution and Urbanization brought significant benefits to Norway. The growth of industry and urbanization led to increased economic prosperity, improved living conditions, and the development of new cultural and artistic expressions. The country's strong social welfare system, developed in the early 20th century, helped to mitigate some of the negative effects of industrialization, and it remains an important part of Norwegian society today.

Overall, the Industrial Revolution and Urbanization had a profound impact on Norway and its history. This period of rapid economic growth and urbanization brought significant changes to the country's economy, society, and culture, and it helped to shape the country's modern identity and culture. While there were significant challenges associated with this period of rapid change, the benefits were also significant, and the legacy of the Industrial Revolution and Urbanization continues to be felt in Norway today.

The Birth of Norwegian Literature and Arts

The Birth of Norwegian Literature and Arts can be traced back to the Romantic Nationalism movement of the 19th century. This cultural movement emphasized the importance of individual freedom, national pride, and cultural expression, and it celebrated the unique history and traditions of each nation.

One of the most important figures in the development of Norwegian literature and arts was the writer Henrik Wergeland. Wergeland was a poet and playwright who celebrated Norwegian history, culture, and language in his works. He was a fierce advocate for the rights of the Norwegian people, and he helped to inspire a sense of national pride and identity among his fellow countrymen. Wergeland's works helped to create a distinct Norwegian literary identity, and his legacy can still be felt in Norwegian literature and culture today.

Another important figure in the development of Norwegian literature and arts was the composer Edvard Grieg. Grieg's music was heavily influenced by Norwegian folk traditions, and it helped to create a distinct Norwegian musical identity. His music celebrated the natural beauty of Norway and the country's unique cultural heritage, and it helped to shape the way that Norwegians thought about themselves and their place in the world.

In addition to literature and music, the Romantic Nationalism movement also had a significant impact on other forms of artistic expression in Norway. This period saw the development of new forms of visual art, such as landscape painting, which celebrated the natural beauty of the Norwegian landscape. The country's natural beauty also inspired new forms of architecture, as artists and designers sought to incorporate the natural environment into their works.

The development of Norwegian literature and arts was also closely tied to the country's struggle for independence from Sweden. The Romantic Nationalism movement played an important role in shaping Norwegian culture and identity, and it helped to inspire a sense of national pride and independence. This cultural movement helped to create a distinct Norwegian identity and culture, and it continues to be an important part of Norwegian society today.

Overall, the Birth of Norwegian Literature and Arts was a significant moment in the country's history. The Romantic Nationalism movement helped to create a distinct Norwegian cultural identity, and it inspired a sense of national pride and independence among the Norwegian people. The legacy of this movement can still be felt in Norwegian literature, music, and arts, and it continues to be an important part of the country's cultural heritage.

The Sami People and Their Struggle for Rights

The Sami people are the indigenous people of Norway, Sweden, Finland, and Russia. The Sami have a unique culture and language, and they have lived in the region for thousands of years. Despite their long history in the region, the Sami people have faced a long struggle for recognition and rights.

For many years, the Sami people were subject to discrimination and marginalization by the majority population. They were often forced to abandon their traditional way of life and assimilate into the dominant culture. In Norway, for example, Sami children were often taken from their families and sent to boarding schools, where they were taught to speak Norwegian and abandon their traditional Sami culture.

In recent years, however, the Sami people have made significant progress in their struggle for recognition and rights. In Norway, the Sami Parliament was established in 1989, giving the Sami people a degree of political representation and self-governance. The Sami Parliament has the power to make decisions about issues such as education, healthcare, and natural resource management.

In addition to political representation, the Sami people have also fought for the recognition of their language and culture. In 1988, the Norwegian government recognized the Sami language as an official language of the country. Today, efforts are underway to revitalize and preserve the Sami language and culture, including through the establishment of Sami-language schools and cultural centers.

Despite these positive developments, the Sami people still face significant challenges in their struggle for rights and recognition. Many Sami people still face discrimination and marginalization, particularly in areas such as employment and access to healthcare. There are also ongoing debates about issues such as land rights and resource management, as the Sami people seek to protect their traditional territories and livelihoods.

Overall, the Sami people and their struggle for rights are an important part of Norway's history and culture. While progress has been made in recent years, there is still much work to be done to ensure that the Sami people are fully recognized and respected as an integral part of Norwegian society. The Sami people and their unique culture and language are an important part of Norway's cultural heritage, and they must be protected and preserved for future generations.

Norway's Role in World War I

Norway remained neutral during World War I, a decision that was made in order to protect the country's interests and maintain its position as a neutral nation. Despite this, Norway was still affected by the war in a number of ways.

One of the most significant ways that Norway was affected by the war was through its role as a neutral shipping nation. Norway's merchant fleet played a vital role in transporting goods and resources between countries during the war, and Norway became one of the world's leading shipping nations as a result. However, this also made Norway vulnerable to attacks from both sides of the conflict. Norwegian ships were often seized or sunk by German U-boats, which caused significant economic losses for the country.

In addition to its shipping industry, Norway also played a role in the war as a supplier of key resources. Norway was one of the world's leading producers of copper, which was a crucial resource for the war effort. The country also exported fish, timber, and other resources that were in high demand during the war.

Despite its neutrality, Norway was not completely isolated from the conflict. The country's relations with its neighboring countries, particularly Germany and Great Britain, were strained during the war. There were also incidents of espionage and sabotage in Norway, as both sides sought to gain an advantage in the conflict.

Overall, Norway's role in World War I was defined by its position as a neutral nation. While the country did not take an active role in the conflict, it was still affected by the war in a number of ways. Norway's merchant fleet played a vital role in the war effort, but the country also suffered significant economic losses as a result of attacks on its shipping industry. The war also had an impact on Norway's relations with other countries, and the country was not immune to incidents of espionage and sabotage during the conflict.

The Interwar Period and the Rise of Fascism

The interwar period between World War I and World War II was a tumultuous time in Norway's history, marked by economic instability, political polarization, and the rise of fascism in Europe. During this time, Norway experienced a period of political and social change that would shape the country for years to come.

One of the most significant factors shaping the interwar period in Norway was the economic crisis that followed World War I. The country's economy was heavily reliant on its shipping industry, which suffered significant losses during the war. This, combined with a global economic downturn, led to widespread unemployment and financial instability throughout the country.

The economic crisis also contributed to political polarization in Norway, as different factions within the country's political parties and labor movement offered competing visions for how to address the crisis. This was particularly evident in the growing divide between the labor movement and the business community, with the former calling for greater social and economic reforms while the latter sought to maintain the status quo.

Amidst this instability, fascist and nationalist movements began to gain traction in Norway. The Norwegian fascist party, Nasjonal Samling (National Unity), was founded in 1933 and quickly gained a following among disaffected segments of the population. The party's leader, Vidkun

Quisling, would later collaborate with the Nazi regime in Germany during World War II.

The rise of fascism in Norway was not limited to political parties, however. The country also experienced a surge in nationalist sentiment during this time, with many Norwegians calling for greater emphasis on Norwegian culture and identity. This was evident in the growing popularity of the Norwegian language and traditional folk customs, as well as in the push for greater autonomy and self-determination for Norway.

Despite the rise of fascism and nationalism in Norway, the country ultimately remained committed to its democratic values and institutions. In the years leading up to World War II, Norway played an active role in promoting international peace and disarmament, and the country remained neutral for the early years of the war. Ultimately, however, Norway would be drawn into the conflict as a result of the Nazi invasion in 1940.

The interwar period in Norway was a time of great change and uncertainty, as the country navigated a period of economic instability and political polarization. The rise of fascism and nationalism presented a significant challenge to Norway's democratic institutions and values, but ultimately the country remained committed to its democratic principles and played an important role in promoting international peace and cooperation during this difficult time.

The German Occupation of Norway during World War II

The German occupation of Norway during World War II was a dark period in the country's history, marked by oppression, resistance, and collaboration. The occupation began on April 9, 1940, when German forces invaded Norway and quickly overran the country's defenses.

The German occupation had a significant impact on every aspect of Norwegian life, from politics and economy to culture and society. The occupying forces established a puppet government under Vidkun Quisling, who had previously led the Norwegian fascist party. The government was largely powerless, however, as the real power rested with the German authorities.

The occupation was characterized by oppression and brutality, with the German authorities employing a range of tactics to maintain control over the population. These included curfews, censorship, and restrictions on freedom of speech and movement. The German authorities also carried out widespread arrests and deportations, targeting individuals and groups seen as threats to their rule.

Despite the oppression, however, there was also resistance. The Norwegian resistance movement was formed shortly after the occupation began, and it played an important role in disrupting German operations and gathering intelligence for the Allied powers. Resistance fighters carried out sabotage and guerrilla operations, and they provided assistance to Allied personnel who were trapped behind enemy lines.

The occupation also had a significant impact on the economy, as the German authorities sought to exploit Norway's resources for their own purposes. Norway's shipping industry was particularly affected, as the Germans seized Norwegian ships and used them for their own war effort. The occupation also had a devastating impact on the country's Jewish population, as the Germans carried out a campaign of persecution and deportation that resulted in the deaths of hundreds of Norwegian Jews.

Collaboration with the German authorities was also a significant issue during the occupation, with some Norwegians choosing to work with the Germans in exchange for personal gain or protection. Collaboration took many forms, from working for the puppet government to joining the Norwegian SS division that fought on the Eastern Front.

The German occupation of Norway was a dark chapter in the country's history, marked by oppression, resistance, and collaboration. The occupation had a significant impact on every aspect of Norwegian life, and it would take many years for the country to recover from the trauma of this period. Nonetheless, the resistance movement and the courage of those who stood up to the occupation serve as a reminder of the resilience and determination of the Norwegian people in the face of adversity.

The Norwegian Resistance Movement

The Norwegian resistance movement during World War II was a critical force in the fight against German occupation and oppression. The resistance was formed shortly after the occupation began in 1940, and it played an important role in disrupting German operations and gathering intelligence for the Allied powers.

The resistance movement was made up of a diverse group of individuals and organizations, united by their opposition to the German occupation. Some resistance fighters were former soldiers or members of the Norwegian military, while others were ordinary citizens who had been radicalized by the oppression they experienced under the occupation.

Resistance activities included sabotage and guerrilla operations, as well as providing assistance to Allied personnel who were trapped behind enemy lines. Sabotage operations targeted key infrastructure and transportation systems, with the goal of disrupting German supply lines and hampering their ability to carry out military operations.

The resistance also played a critical role in gathering intelligence for the Allied powers, providing information on German troop movements, supply lines, and other important military operations. This information was often transmitted to the Allied powers via radio or other covert means, and it was used to plan military operations and coordinate strategic decisions.

One of the most significant actions taken by the resistance was the sinking of the German heavy water production facility at Vemork in 1943. This facility was a key component in the German nuclear program, and its destruction was a major setback for the Germans.

The resistance movement faced significant challenges during the occupation, including the threat of arrest and execution by the German authorities. Resistance fighters often operated in secrecy, using aliases and covert communication methods to avoid detection.

Despite these challenges, however, the resistance movement continued to grow throughout the occupation. Resistance fighters were inspired by the bravery and determination of their comrades, and they remained committed to the cause of liberating Norway from German occupation.

The Norwegian resistance movement played a critical role in the fight against German occupation during World War II. Its members risked their lives to disrupt German operations, gather intelligence, and provide assistance to Allied personnel. The resistance movement remains a symbol of courage and determination, and it serves as a reminder of the power of ordinary citizens to resist oppression and fight for their freedom.

The Post-War Reconstruction and Social Democracy

The post-war reconstruction of Norway was a challenging but ultimately successful period in the country's history. In the aftermath of World War II, Norway faced significant economic and social challenges, including widespread destruction of infrastructure and a shortage of resources.

To address these challenges, the Norwegian government implemented a range of policies aimed at rebuilding the country's economy and improving the standard of living for its citizens. These policies were rooted in the principles of social democracy, which emphasized social welfare programs and government intervention in the economy.

One of the most significant policies implemented during this period was the establishment of the welfare state. This system provided a range of benefits and services to Norwegian citizens, including universal healthcare, free education, and a strong social safety net. The welfare state was intended to reduce poverty and promote social equality, and it played a critical role in improving the quality of life for Norwegians in the post-war period.

Another important aspect of the post-war reconstruction was the rebuilding of infrastructure. Much of Norway's transportation and communication networks had been destroyed during the war, and significant investments were needed to rebuild these systems. The government also invested in housing, particularly in urban areas where there was a shortage of affordable housing.

The post-war period also saw the development of Norway's oil industry, which would become a major source of economic growth and development in the decades that followed. The discovery of oil in the North Sea in the late 1960s and early 1970s provided Norway with a significant source of income, and the government used this revenue to fund social welfare programs and infrastructure projects.

The principles of social democracy that guided the post-war reconstruction period continue to play a significant role in Norwegian politics and society today. Norway is consistently ranked as one of the happiest and most prosperous countries in the world, and its success can be attributed in part to the social welfare programs and government intervention in the economy that were established during the post-war period.

Overall, the post-war reconstruction of Norway was a challenging but ultimately successful period in the country's history. The government's focus on social welfare programs, infrastructure investment, and economic development laid the foundation for the country's prosperity and social equality in the decades that followed.

The Discovery of Oil and the Norwegian Economic Miracle

The discovery of oil in the North Sea in the late 1960s and early 1970s was a pivotal moment in Norwegian history, and it would have a significant impact on the country's economy and society for decades to come.

Before the discovery of oil, Norway was a largely agrarian economy with limited natural resources. However, the oil boom transformed the country into one of the wealthiest and most prosperous in the world.

Initially, the Norwegian government took a cautious approach to oil development, wary of the potential environmental risks and concerned about the impact that oil revenues might have on the economy. However, as the potential economic benefits became clear, the government began to embrace the oil industry, establishing a state-owned oil company, Statoil, and investing heavily in infrastructure and technology to support the industry.

One of the most significant benefits of the oil boom was the revenue it generated for the Norwegian government. The country established a sovereign wealth fund, the Government Pension Fund Global, which is now one of the largest in the world. The fund is designed to provide for the country's long-term economic needs, and it has helped to insulate the Norwegian economy from the volatility of the oil market.

The oil boom also had a significant impact on Norway's society and culture. The newfound wealth allowed the country to invest heavily in social welfare programs, infrastructure, and education, and Norway is now widely regarded as one of the most socially progressive countries in the world.

Despite the economic benefits of the oil industry, there have also been some challenges. One of the most significant concerns has been the environmental impact of oil drilling and exploration. The Norwegian government has taken steps to address these concerns, implementing strict regulations and investing in research and development to reduce the environmental impact of the industry.

Overall, the discovery of oil in the North Sea was a transformative moment in Norwegian history. It allowed the country to become one of the wealthiest and most prosperous in the world, and it had a significant impact on the country's society and culture. While there have been challenges associated with the oil industry, Norway's approach to managing its oil resources has been widely praised as a model for responsible and sustainable development.

The Expansion of the Welfare State and Social Progressivism

The expansion of the welfare state and social progressivism in Norway has been a central feature of the country's modern history. Beginning in the post-World War II period, the Norwegian government has implemented a series of policies designed to promote social equality and provide for the needs of its citizens.

One of the key elements of the Norwegian welfare state is the provision of universal healthcare. Norway has a publicly funded healthcare system that provides free or low-cost medical care to all residents. The system is funded through taxes and is designed to ensure that everyone has access to high-quality healthcare, regardless of their income or social status.

In addition to healthcare, the Norwegian government provides a wide range of social services and benefits to its citizens. This includes free education at all levels, including university, as well as generous maternity and paternity leave policies, subsidized childcare, and public pensions. The government also provides support for low-income families, including housing subsidies and food assistance programs.

One of the unique features of the Norwegian welfare state is its emphasis on social equality and the redistribution of wealth. The government has implemented a progressive tax system that ensures that the wealthiest citizens pay a higher percentage of their income in taxes, while providing more benefits and services to those in need. This approach has helped to create a more equal and just society, with lower levels of income inequality than many other developed countries.

The expansion of the welfare state in Norway has been accompanied by a broader shift towards social progressivism. This has included the legalization of same-sex marriage and adoption, the decriminalization of drug use, and the adoption of policies designed to promote gender equality and protect the rights of minorities.

Overall, the expansion of the welfare state and social progressivism in Norway has been a defining feature of the country's modern history. It has helped to create a more equal and just society, and has ensured that all citizens have access to high-quality healthcare, education, and social services. While there are certainly challenges associated with the welfare state, including the cost of providing these services, Norway's approach to social welfare is widely regarded as a model for other countries to follow.

The Norwegian Model of Democracy and Diplomacy

The Norwegian model of democracy and diplomacy is often cited as a model for other countries to follow. It is characterized by a strong commitment to democracy, human rights, and international cooperation.

Norway's democracy is based on a parliamentary system, with a strong tradition of political consensus building. This approach is reflected in the Norwegian system of government, which is characterized by a high degree of cooperation between political parties and a commitment to finding common ground on important issues.

Norway is also known for its commitment to human rights, both domestically and internationally. The country has a strong legal framework for protecting human rights, including laws against discrimination and hate speech, and has been a vocal advocate for human rights on the global stage.

In terms of diplomacy, Norway is known for its commitment to international cooperation and conflict resolution. The country is a strong supporter of the United Nations, and has played an active role in peacekeeping and conflict resolution efforts around the world. Norway is also a major donor of foreign aid, and has been recognized for its efforts to promote sustainable development in developing countries.

One of the key features of Norway's diplomatic approach is its focus on dialogue and engagement. Rather than relying on coercion or force, Norway seeks to build relationships and find common ground with other countries. This approach has been particularly evident in Norway's efforts to broker peace agreements in the Middle East and in Sri Lanka.

Norway is also known for its commitment to environmental sustainability and its efforts to address climate change. The country has a strong track record of environmental protection, and has been a leader in promoting sustainable development and green technology.

Overall, the Norwegian model of democracy and diplomacy is characterized by a strong commitment to democracy, human rights, and international cooperation. Through its diplomatic efforts, Norway has sought to promote peace, stability, and sustainable development around the world, and has been recognized for its leadership on a range of global issues.

Contemporary Norway: Challenges and Prospects

Contemporary Norway faces a number of challenges and opportunities as it navigates the complex landscape of the 21st century. While the country has made significant progress in areas such as social welfare, environmental protection, and human rights, it continues to face challenges related to immigration, economic inequality, and geopolitical uncertainty.

One of the major challenges facing contemporary Norway is immigration. Like many other Western countries, Norway has experienced a significant influx of immigrants in recent decades, leading to debates over issues such as cultural integration, social welfare, and national identity. While Norway has a reputation for being welcoming to refugees and immigrants, the country has also struggled to find a balance between supporting diversity and preserving its own cultural traditions.

Economic inequality is another challenge facing Norway. While the country has one of the highest standards of living in the world, there are still significant disparities between the wealthy and the less fortunate. This has led to debates over issues such as taxation, social welfare, and access to healthcare, with some arguing that Norway needs to do more to address these inequalities in order to maintain its position as a global leader in social progressivism.

Geopolitical uncertainty is also a concern for Norway. The country's close relationship with the European Union has been called into question in recent years, as the EU has faced a number of challenges related to economic instability, political fragmentation, and migration. At the same time, Norway has had to navigate complex relationships with countries such as Russia and the United States, which have at times been strained by issues such as energy security and security policy.

Despite these challenges, there are also a number of opportunities for Norway in the coming years. The country's leadership in areas such as renewable energy, sustainable development, and peacebuilding offer potential for continued global influence and impact. Norway's commitment to international cooperation and diplomacy also provides a strong foundation for addressing the many challenges facing the world today.

In addition, Norway's tradition of political consensus building and strong social welfare system offer a model for other countries looking to address issues such as economic inequality and social justice. As the world continues to evolve and face new challenges, Norway will likely continue to play an important role in shaping global conversations and driving positive change.

Conclusion

After exploring the rich history of Norway, it is clear that the country has undergone significant changes throughout the centuries. From the early inhabitants and the Viking Age, to the Christianization and the Union with Sweden, Norway has constantly evolved and adapted to new circumstances.

The discovery of oil in the North Sea in the 1960s sparked an economic miracle, which allowed Norway to expand its welfare state and become a prosperous country with a high standard of living. The Norwegian Model of Democracy and Diplomacy, which emphasizes consensus and cooperation, has also become a notable feature of the country's political landscape.

However, contemporary Norway faces its own set of challenges, including increasing social inequality, climate change, and the integration of refugees and immigrants. It remains to be seen how the country will navigate these issues in the coming years.

Despite its challenges, Norway's rich history and cultural heritage continue to inspire and fascinate people around the world. Its stunning natural scenery, vibrant cities, and unique traditions make it a truly special place, and its people have demonstrated resilience and adaptability throughout the centuries.

As we look to the future, it is important to remember the lessons of the past and continue to build upon Norway's remarkable legacy. With its strong commitment to democracy, social progressivism, and environmental sustainability, Norway has the potential to remain a global leader and inspire positive change for generations to come.

Thank you for taking the time to read this book on the history of Norway. We hope that it has provided you with a deeper understanding and appreciation of this fascinating country and its people.

If you enjoyed the book and found it informative, we would greatly appreciate it if you could leave a positive review on your preferred platform. Your feedback helps us to continue to improve and create more engaging content in the future.

Thank you once again for your support, and we hope that you continue to explore the rich history and culture of Norway.